THE

PILGRIMS AND THE PURITANS:

THEIR

PRINCIPLES, CHARACTER, AND POWER.

BY

GEORGE B. CHEEVER, D.D.

THE INHERITANCE OF PRINCIPLES, CHARACTER, AND POWER RECEIVED FROM OUR PILGRIM AND PURITAN ANCESTORS, AND THE ONLY MEANS OF PERPETUATING IT.

A DISCOURSE,

PREACHED DEC. 22, 1850,

IN

THE CHURCH OF THE PURITANS,

ON OCCASION OF

The Anniversary of the Landing of our Pilgrim Fathers.

BY

GEORGE B. CHEEVER, D.D.

NEW YORK:

JOHN WILEY, 304 BROADWAY.

1851.

S. W. BENEDICT,
Printer, 16 Spruce-Street.

DISCOURSE.

MALACHI, 4: 6. And he shall turn the heart of the fathers to the children, and the heart of the children to their fathers, lest I come and smite the earth with a curse.

TAKING these words as intimating an admiration and imitation of the holy fathers of the nation, and a return to the love and practice of their faith and virtue, nothing can be more suitable on the present occasion. We are to dwell upon the principles and character of our Pilgrim and Puritan Fathers, and the inheritance of power and responsibility growing out of it.

Principles, Character, Power! Character grows out of principles, principles are the foundation and the beams of character, and character wrought out of virtuous principles is the source of power. Then power increases by Divine Grace and Providence, and by an internal necessity and law of progress, as long as the vital inspiring principles continue. All our good institutions received a momentum from the force of character and principle, with which our fathers set them a-going, that is carrying them on still. And onward they will go, over all obstacles, if we are but faithful to our fathers, and our father's God.

I remark as the first and greatest point to be considered in the character of our Pilgrim and Puritan ancestors, their unquestionable and remarkable piety. They had a most submissive and unwavering trust in God. They drew their motives from on high. They beheld the throne of God, and the powers of the world to come took fast hold upon them.

The whole class of loftiest Christian graces and virtues was singularly predominant in the development of their character and life. Faith, hope, love, forbearance, self-denying endurance, indomitable perseverance; and all these things for God and His glory, not self or self-aggrandisement. Their piety was deep and self-forgetting, and they had no private schemes. From the first moment of their setting out in the Christian life, at such a period of persecution as then prevailed in England, they were weaned from the world, and raised above it, by the very tempests that beat upon them.

> The whirlwinds that rise
> Shall gloriously hurry our souls to the skies.

Men who became Christians at all, in such a period, must of necessity, be so rooted, as in time of persecution not to fall away. Perhaps the earliest church ever founded on these principles in modern times was in 1592, in London, when fifty-six of its members were hunted out by Queen Elizabeth's Commissioners, and put to death by various inhuman cruelties. These martyred children of God, when they refused to go to the State-church, as commanded by law to do, were told by the Commissioners that it was not piety to God that was required of them, but obedience to the Queen, and that "if they would only come to the Established Church, and obey the Queen's laws, they might be dissemblers, hypocrites, or devils, if they would." So much regard for religion the kingdoms and princes of this world generally have had, when, under pretence of rendering unto Cæsar the things that are Cæsar's, they have forbidden men to render unto God the things that are God's. Away with your religion from politics, has been the cry. Religion is a good thing everywhere else, but in politics it makes men mad.

Ten years after this, in 1602, a few Christian persons on the borders of Lincolnshire, whom God had taught by his spirit, joined themselves by covenant into a church, "as the Lord's free people." The preceding persecutions had been God's window, to let light into their souls, and they had come to the conclusion, in their own words,"that the ceremonies prescribed were unlawful, and also the lordly and tyrannous power of the prelates, who would, contrary to the freedom of the gospel, load the consciences of men, and by their compulsive power make a profane mixture of things and persons in divine worship; that their offices, courts, and canons, were unlawful, being such as have no warrant in the Word of God, but the same that were used in Popery, and still retained." Out of that church covenant grew the civil and religious constitution formed near twenty years afterward on board the May Flower, formed on God's highway, under no human jurisdiction, within no human empire, neither the outgrowth, nor appendage, nor codicil, nor consequence, of any other constitution on earth, but a legitimate result of that free New Testament Church Covenant, in which were the germs and the spirit of all the civil and religious freedom in our country.

And now we beg you to remark, as a thing worthy of solemn note at this present time in our land, that this church covenant, out of which God has caused to spring the freest constitutions, the most religious states, and the mightiest growing empire in the world, *was itself the direct product of disobedience to unrighteous human law.* It grew out of the conviction that the things prescribed and forced upon them by human law were unlawful in the sight of God, having no warrant in his Word, and not to be obeyed by his people. Had it not been for this conviction, and a conscientious, correspondent, resolute action in carrying it out, throwing themselves solely upon God for his protection, the May Flower would never have borne that band of Pilgrims on a stormy sea, nor ever witnessed the signing of that constitution of freedom, which was the foundation of all our liberties.

That Constitution sets forth as its very first objects the glory of God and advancement of the Christian Faith, and for those ends they entered into that Covenant, by virtue of it constituting themselves a civil body politic, "to enact, constitute and frame such just and equal laws, ordinances, acts, constitutions, offices, from time to time, as shall be thought most meet and convenient for the general good of the Colony; unto which we promise all due submission and obedience." Let the care be marked, with which, in the first place, they made the glory of God their supreme law and object; in the second place, determined to enact such laws only as were just and equal, the supreme and only infallible judge of such justice and equality being, in their view, God's Word; and in the third place, bound themselves to render all *due* submission and obedience, and that only. They would sooner have cut off their right hands than they would have signed a contract to render obedience to human law, any farther than God's Word and their own consciences permitted them to do.

They had signed their Church Covenant "as the Lord's free people, to walk in all his ways, made known, or to be made known to them, according to their best endeavors, *whatever it might cost them.*" A tremendous sentence was that, levelling a blow right at the gates of hell, stronger than had been struck for centuries, but involving also for themselves an amount of toil, hardship, suffering, privation, persecution, and sorrow even unto death, of which, with all their familiarity even then with trial, they could hardly dream. At whatever cost! O noble spirit! And it was indeed a mighty cost, involving the sacrifice of all that we hold dear on earth, ease, comfort, friends, a quiet fireside, their country and their homes. But what were all these blessings, to souls trained, inspired, and taught of God as they were, without freedom of opinion and of conscience? Their very Church Covenant was in itself the absolute insurance of persecution and malignity on the part of the world and the world's law ; but God had disciplined them for their great work, by a baptism of affliction beneath the oppression of unjust human law, that they might have, to the last moment of life, an indomitable spirit of civil and religious freedom. It was the flail of persecution that first beat them out from the Established Church, and separated the chaff from the wheat, and then God suffered them to be ground between the millstones of civil and ecclesiastical despotism, that they might come out the finest and purest of the flour.

Now we can hardly conceive the extent of our obligations to their sufferings, and to the spirit of their determined, conscientious, patient, passive, but enduring and energetic resistance to oppressive law. We are hardly able to conceive the extent to which the whole world, almost, was steeped in the spirit and maxims of despotism. The will of the monarch was regarded as supreme. And even in our own day, though the thing is absolutely ludicrous, a grave charge has been brought by distinguished historians against our Pilgrim Fathers, because they had the audacity to choose for their church in America an independent New Testament form, in opposition to what they knew to be the sentiments and worship of the King! Though the accusation is but the record of a virtue, yet the excellent historian (Grahame) thinks it worth while to defend the memory of the Pilgrims against such charges, and devotes several of his pages to their refutation.

Neither can we adequately conceive what the whole world owes to our Pilgrim and Puritan Fathers. An empire of freedom in self-government was to be founded, in reliance upon God, and under the guidance of his word. It could not come into existence at once, for the world was not prepared for it; and it must grow out of the practice of hardship, self-denial, and self-government, generation after generation, for more than a hundred years, before it could begin, either by example or by power, to have an effect upon the nations. *Now*, it rouses the world. More than two hundred years after the first band and generation of toiling, praying, dying patriots had gone to their graves, (quiet graves in the wilderness, how wild, how peaceful, uncovenanted with man, but covenanted with God, and watched for the resurrection,) it shakes the empires of the whole earth to their centre. There is not a despotic government on earth, nor an Anti-Christian hierarchy, but trembles and totters before it.

But if all this mighty influence had come suddenly, it would have been as a devastating earthquake or volcano; and therefore God caused it to grow up gradually, almost silently, by his providence and grace, and the nations, if they please, may all grow wiser and happier by this very power. But if this experiment had failed, the whole world must have gone back to tyranny, and would now have been more filled with misery and crime than at any time in the last hundred years. The throes of liberty, even in the French Revolution, would not have been experienced; in all probability, no incarnation of individual ambition and power like Napoleon, would have been raised up to drive God's ploughshare of convulsion and of preparation fiercely over Europe, no new examples, or movements, or structures, or lessons, of human freedom would have arisen, and so far as we can judge, not only religion, but science and invention itself, would have cast the shadow of their dial backward.

Such is our inheritance of character and principles, and of power growing out of them. But we must look more particularly at some of the forms in which these possessions are enshrined, and under which, and by the perpetuated purity of which alone it is, that the glory of freedom can continue with ourselves, or an ennobling and redeeming influence go forth from us upon the nations. And the first thing I shall mention is the SABBATH OF OUR GOD, of the true holiness of which, the Puritans held almost the first true scriptural and spiritual conception; and of the holy observance of which they set almost the very first example, that had been known on earth for more than a thousand years. And here again, they gained this glorious possession, accomplished this victory, and made this marked advancement in the Kingdom of God, by a faithful determined disobedience of unrighteous human laws, even unto death. They rescued the Sabbath from the profanation of popular immorality, and the desecration of iniquitous civil and ecclesiastical statutes, and gave their heart, life, and worship to it, as the Day of God. The desecration of the Sabbath in Holland was one of the grand reasons constraining the Pilgrims to leave their quiet abode as a church in Leyden. And in England, at the same time, by the laws of a drunken King, the ministers of Christ were ordered to read in the churches proclamations for dancing, archery, leaping, vaulting, May-games, May-poles, and other sports upon the Sabbath, as a special privilege and reward for those who attended the Established Church; and whoever had loyalty enough to his God and Saviour to refuse to read these blasphemous edicts, was forthwith suspended and imprisoned.

Now by the principles promulgated in some quarters in our day, these ministers of God were all bound to obey these laws of man to the letter, asking no questions for conscience sake; and if they refused to obey them, they went against the ordinance of God commanding obedience to the powers that be. According to the theories even of some professedly religious men, those holy and noble spirits, who cast defiance at King James and his Book of Sports, and refused to obey his laws for profaning God's day, were setting to the people an example of treason and rebellion! For if you say that this forms an exception, because one of God's explicit laws is, "Thou shalt honor the Sabbath day to keep it holy," the answer is plain, that the King and his laws contemplated that very thing; contemplated the keeping the Sabbath in the very way they asserted to be right, that is, by sports and dances. And who are you, ask these venal theorists, that pretend to set up your conscience against human law, as to the manner of keeping the Sabbath? If the powers that be, command you to keep it by sports and dances, then that command makes that manner of keeping it right; for that which would have been wrong, tried by the word of God, becomes right when human law authorises it. Such is the iniquitous sophistry which has been in some quarters recently palmed upon the people; such is the immoral casuistry, by which, could it be successful, the authority of God's word would most certainly be destroyed, and infidelity, wide-spreading and resistless, would take its place among the nations.

It has been sometimes said that the inevitable recoil of holy prayerful minds from such abominable examples and laws of licentiousness for the profanation of God's holy day, threw back the Puritans into a legality and over-strictness in the observance of it, rather suited to the genius of the Jewish, than of the Christian dispensation. But they were laying the foundations of many generations, and would to God we had the Puritan Sabbath, in all its strictness, back again, over the whole length and breadth of our land. It is impossible that the Puritan institutions of freedom can be sustained, if the Puritan Sabbath goes down; for the Puritan Sabbath was the Sabbath of God, and in the main it was kept by our fathers, as it was for many happy years by their descendants, and is now to a good degree, better at least than any where else on earth, in the main, as God would have it. If they erred at all, they *ought* to err upon the side of strictness. The descendants of the Pilgrims are as yet a Sabbath-keeping people, and none but a Sabbath-keeping people can be truly free. Our fathers were almost theocratists; they were entirely so in all things relating to religious duty, and so we all ought to be. They took God's law as their law, God as their King, and to him they were loyal. For the bright example they set to the world in this matter of keeping the Sabbath, if for nothing else, their memory would deserve to be enshrined with admiring love in the soul of every Christian patriot. They so acted in this thing, that the whole world might safely imitate them. Their very first Sabbath was a glory to their life, and a light to all generations; for though within ten minutes sail, if the wind and tide favored, of the place where they were to abide all the rest of their pilgrimage, they moored amidst the nipping cold, at a desolate island, and would not again set a sail that day, nor take an oar in hand, nor do aught of worldly work, because it was the Lord's Day, and they dedicated its hours to the worship of their God. It was the beginning of their perfect freedom from bondage, and it was a wonderful consecration of all New England to God, when there they raised their Sabbath hymns and Sabbath prayers.

> Amidst the storm they sang,
> And the stars heard, and the sea,
> And the sounding aisles of the dim woods rang
> To the anthems of the free.

And now if you wish to bring back bondage instead of freedom, the fear of man instead of the love of God, superstition instead of religion, licentiousness instead of virtue, immorality instead of piety, bring back the European and the Romish Sabbath! Parade the streets with processions to the sound of military music; suffer the shops for intoxicating drink to be open on the Sabbath Day, and the law for its protection to be shamelessly violated; employ your vagrant boys in the sale of immoral newspapers, making the Sabbath their day of profitable trade; open the theatres on Sabbath evening, commencing by the mask and pretence of concerts of sacred operatic music; let intrusion after intrusion be made upon the sacredness of the day with impunity, and while you invoke the majesty of law to protect your own property, let the laws framed for rendering unto God the things that are God's sleep as a dead letter; do all this, and suffer all this, and step after step religion will decline, and luxury, effeminacy, corruption, venality, and the worship of wealth and power, will come in, and the principles that alone can perpetuate our freedom will die out of existence.

But by God's grace this shall never be. By God's grace we will hold on to the Puritan Sabbath, and in so doing we will preserve and perpetuate another possession of our Pilgrim fathers, priceless and glorious, THE INDEPENDENCE AND FREEDOM OF THE PULPIT. Perhaps in no country on earth has the pulpit been so free and outspoken for a series of generations, as in this country; so directly connected with God's throne, so entirely independent of human statutes and influences. Our memory of the Latimers, the Baxters, the Bunyans of England, and other noble Puritans, amidst the sacred baptism of fiery persecution, presents periods of unrivalled plainness, boldness, and independence there also; but nowhere on earth is independence and freedom of opinion and of speech a possession of the ministry so characteristic, habitual, admitted and expected, as in this country. And no language can tell the importance of preserving this independence. God will sustain it, if He means to make preaching the grand instrumentality for converting the world. The pulpit is a sacred, free, exalted enshrinement of all God's messages to our fallen race. All institutions are beneath it; it is far above all earthly things. It is superior alike to the despotism of public opinion, and the petty tyranny of individual minds. It ought ever to guide public opinion, and not follow it. A time-serving pulpit is one of the greatest evils God ever suffers to fall upon a people. In our day, beyond all question, the pulpit is too apt to follow in the wake of the merchants and the newspapers, and to regard not only what God says in his word, and what will meet God's approbation, but also what will meet the sanction of the exchange, and the approbation of the public press. Popularity is the element which the Pulpit is in danger of courting, instead of manifesting an independent faithfulness to God's word and to the souls of men. This is a great crippling of its power. The extreme of this evil was one of the grand causes of ancient Israel's overthrow. The priests preached at the bidding of the princes, and of the rulers, and of the people, what would please *them*, not what was in God's word. You have in the seventh chapter of the Prophecy of Amos a conflict between a time-serving priest and one of God's most resolute and faithful prophets, with the terrible thunderbolt of God's wrath because his word was restrained and slighted.

The prophet Amos had been commissioned to declare both to Israel and Judah the indignation of the Lord because of their iniquities; "because they have despised the law of the Lord, and have not kept his commandments, but their lies caused them to err, after the which their fathers have walked; because they sold the righteous for silver, and the poor for a pair of shoes; because they oppressed the poor, and crushed the needy, but said to their masters, Bring, and let us drink together! They hate him that rebuketh in the gate, and they abhor him that speaketh uprightly. They afflict the just, they take a bribe, and they turn aside the poor in the gate from their right. Therefore the high places of Isaac shall be desolate, and the sanctuaries of Israel shall be laid waste; and I will rise against the house of Jeroboam with a sword."

Such was the tenor of the message of Amos, and just as God commanded him, so he delivered it, directly against the house of Jeroboam. Then Amaziah, the priest of Bethel, where he himself had charge of King Jeroboam's own chapel, took it upon himself, in his zeal for the powers that be, to accuse Amos of conspiracy and sedition. He sent word to Jeroboam, King of Israel, " saying, Amos hath conspired against thee in the midst of the house of Israel; the land is not able to bear all his words. For thus Amos saith, Jeroboam shall die by the sword, and Israel shall surely be led away captive out of thine own land. Also, Amaziah said unto Amos, O, thou seer, go, flee thee away into the land of Judah, and there eat bread, and prophesy there; but prophesy not again any more at Bethel, *for it is the King's chapel, and it is the King's court.*"

Such was the advice of a venal, time-serving priest, and such his impiety in forbidding the proclamation of the word of the Lord. And now behold the wrath of God in consequence of it.

" Then answered Amos, and said to Amaziah, I was no prophet, neither was I a prophet's son; but I was an herdman, and a gatherer of sycamore fruit; and the Lord took me as I followed the flock, and the Lord said unto me, go, prophesy unto my people Israel. Now therefore, hear *thou* the word of the Lord! Thou sayest, Prophesy not against Israel, and drop not thy word against the house of Isaac. Therefore, thus saith the Lord; Thy wife shall be an harlot in the city, and thy sons and thy daughters shall fall by the sword, and thy land shall be divided by line, and thou shalt die in a polluted land, and Israel shall surely go into captivity forth of his land."

This singular drama is full of character and fire, and it is one of the most solemn, admonitory, and instructive pages in the word of God. It shows with what burning indignation he regards every attempt to prevent the preaching of his word, just as he has given it.

You have also, in the 30th chapter of the Prophecy of Isaiah an example of the height and desperateness to which this wickedness of the refusal of the word of God had risen, and of the devouring anger of the Lord God against it.

"Now go, write it before them in a table, and note it in a book, that it may be for the time to come forever and ever; that this is a rebellious people, lying children, children that will not hear the law of the Lord; which say to the seers, See not; and to the prophets, Prophesy not unto us right things, prophesy smooth things, prophesy deceits, get ye out of the way, turn aside out of the path, cause the Holy One of Israel to cease from before us." This is precisely the iniquity of those who exclaim, Away with religion from politics, and who dare to affirm that there is no higher law than human law for man's guidance under a civil state.

"Wherefore, thus saith the Holy One of Israel, Because ye despise this word, and trust in oppression and perverseness, and stay yourselves thereon, therefore this iniquity shall be to you as a breach ready to fall, swelling out in a high wall, whose breaking cometh suddenly at an instant." The same strain of fiery retribution for the same sins is to be found in all the Prophets, and also in the Psalms. Let any man read the twelve first chapters of the Prophesy of Jeremiah, or the twenty-second and twenty-third chapters of the same, and compare them not only with the sharp words of the minor Prophets, but with the thirteenth and twenty-second chapters of Ezekiel, and he will need no other demonstration of the vengeance of the Lord God against those who would silence his word, or set up laws for man's guidance conflicting with it.

"Shall the throne of iniquity have fellowship with thee, which frameth mischief by a law?" "Ephraim is oppressed and broken, because he willingly walked after the commandment;" that is, the statutes of the house of Ahab. "This saith the Lord (by the mouth of Micah,) concerning the prophets that make my people err, that bite with their teeth, and cry, Peace; and he that putteth not into their mouths, they even prepare war against him; therefore night shall be unto you, that ye shall not have a vision, and it shall be dark unto you, that ye shall not divine, and the sun shall go down over the prophets, and the day shall be dark over them. Then shall the seers be ashamed, and the diviners confounded; yea, they shall all cover their lips, for there is no answer of God."

Then speaks the true and faithful Prophet, in the might and confidence of God, "Truly," he says, "I am full of power by the Spirit of the Lord, and of judgment, and of might, to declare unto Jacob his transgression, and to Israel his sin. Hear this I pray you, ye heads of the house of Jacob, and princes of the house of Israel, that abhor judgment, and pervert all equity; they build up Zion with blood, and Jerusalem with iniquity. The heads thereof judge for reward, and the priests thereof teach for hire, and the prophets thereof divine for money; yet will they lean upon the Lord, and say, is not the Lord among us? none evil can come upon us. Therefore, shall Zion, for your sakes, be ploughed as a field, and Jerusalem shall become heaps, and the mountain of the house as the high places of the forest. *For the statutes of Omri are kept, and all the works of the house of Ahab;* that I should make thee a desolation, and the inhabitants thereof a hissing; therefore ye shall bear the reproach of my people."

Yet, notwithstanding all this, the evil went on increasing, and although God raised up such a series of the Hebrew Prophets, that their words have been an enshrinement of liberty and piety for the whole world, yet, even amidst all their rebukes, there were false prophets, who hearkened to the rulers instead of obeying God, and who prophesied smooth things to the people, making them willing to follow after the unholy commandments enacted for them by thrones of iniquity. It was for this reason that God's wrath came upon them to the uttermost, and he gave them over to statutes of the Pagans that were not good; and as they had preferred to obey the iniquitous rules introduced by Baal-worshipping kings, rather than to obey God, excusing their violation of conscience and of God's word by their pretence of allegiance to the powers that be, God sent the whole nation into a captivity under heathen laws. He sent them to learn at heathen altars, beneath the horrible oppression of blaspheming heathen kings, the consequences of choosing to obey man rather than God. And there, amidst tyranny and persecution, He woke up the ancient spirit of the nation, and produced, amidst the roar of lions in the royal den, and of flames in the fiery furnace, examples of obedience to God and defiance of the authority of man, which have proved ever since a source of life and power to every intrepid spirit, and of terror to every tyrant, and will do so to the last day.

And yet the incurable evil went on, and those whom the princes and the people could not succeed in silencing, they put to death, till God himself caused the voice of the prophets to cease, because they had lost their independence, and catered for human patronage and applause, instead of seeking the divine approbation. Those that did remain faithful were persecuted even to death, till Jerusalem was characterized by the Saviour of the world as the murdering city; thou that killest the prophets, and stonest them that are sent unto thee. And this one mighty sin, the destruction of the independence of the pulpit, and the persecution of God's faithful ambassadors, was charged upon the nation as the grand cause of their destruction. Yet, even then, they were building and gilding the tombs of the prophets. And with an inconsistency which you may see more or less in every age, they cried Alleluia to the faithfulness of those whom their fathers persecuted, while at the very same moment they were plotting the death of the faithful servants of God and preachers of the gospel, and of Christ Jesus himself, right then preaching in the midst of them. Just so now, men will shout their applause of Latimer, Luther, John Huss, John Knox, John Bunyan, and all the martyrs of a former age, but if the same faithfulness were displayed among themselves in a similar conjuncture, would cry, Away with such a fellow from the earth! He teaches nothing but treason and rebellion! And the truth is, if the preferring God's law to man's in all cases where they come in conflict, and the choosing obedience to God rather than man, is to be called treason and rebellion, then all God's faithful ministers are bound to be, and all will be, traitors and rebels to the end of time.

The word of God is not bound, and cannot be bound. It *will* prevail. All things that oppose it shall yet go down before it. It will have irresistible sway. All human opinions and statutes are as grass before it. Sweep, sweep, comes the scythe of God's word, and down goes the whole growth of falsehood. For all flesh is grass, and all the glory of man as the flower of grass. The grass withereth, and the flower thereof falleth away, but the word of the Lord endureth for ever!

Now, when in any way the supremacy of God's Word is called in question, it ought to kindle a holy jealousy in the heart of every one of God's servants. The word of God from that moment becomes as fire in the bones, and *will* break out. When we see worms of the dust, whose breath is in their nostrils, setting up their statutes, and declaring that what without them would be, by God's word, wrong, is by them changed into right, we feel like covering our faces with our hands, and falling down prostrate before God, expecting, like Moses, that the plague has gone out among the people. We are distressed and filled with anguish at such profane sophistry, and we tremble for its results.

Moreover, if there be anything in God's word, which the opinion and interdict of man, or of earthly statute, forbids us from declaring, we feel almost irresistibly impelled to turn the lightning of God's Word directly upon that very thing. We feel called upon to vindicate the insulted majesty of God's law; we must do it. In the name of all that is sacred, to whom shall the people look for instruction from God's word, as to all their moral and religious duties, but to God's ambassadors? "For the priest's lips should keep knowledge, and they should seek the law at his mouth; for he is the messenger of the Lord of Hosts. But ye (God now speaks on in a strain of rebuke for the violation of this command,) but ye are departed out of the way; ye have caused many to stumble at the law; ye have corrupted the covenant of Levi, saith the Lord of Hosts. Therefore have I also made you contemptible and base before all the people, according as ye have not kept my ways, but have been partial in the law. Have we not all one father? hath not one God created us? why do we deal treacherously every man against his brother, by profaning the covenant of our fathers? The Lord will cut off the man that doeth this, the master and the scholar, out of the tabernacles of Jacob, and him that offereth an offering unto the Lord of Hosts."

Now there is nothing so important to be preserved, as an Apostolic, Puritanic independence, boldness, and faithfulness in the Pulpit. There are powerful temptations against it, and there are insidious advances to put it down; but the men who labor to destroy it, could they be successful, would find too late, to their own cost, that they were working to destroy the bulwarks and safeguard of their own and their country's liberties. But God, we trust, will never permit this, and whatever temporary time-serving policy might prevail, you cannot stop human opinion, nor the action of the human conscience, so long as the Word of God is in the world. All the political, material, mercantile, manufacturing, moneyed, and ambitious interests on earth combined, cannot stop human opinion. It *will* be free. It will work, it will seethe, it will ferment, it will roll hither and thither, to and fro, and the more you strive to enclose it, to suffocate it, to put it down, to hush its voice, to repress its agitation, the more it will rage and roar, and go on concentrating its energies, till you and all your safeguards, and all the mountains you have thrown upon it, and all the structures you have built in imagined safety on the sides of those mountains, are blown into the air, and scattered in ten thousand ruins. You might as well build a country seat for safety over the mouth of Etna. And when conscience comes in as an element, and based upon, and regulated and instructed by God's Word, is the guiding element, the whole world of despotism is impotent before it. Your tyrants are dumb and helpless, both ecclesiastical and civil, the moment you put conscience into God's keeping, not man's.

And hence the iniquity of those who, in order to get conscience under political management, dare to insinuate and maintain that after all the Word of God is not very plain as to specific human duty, that it leaves men very much in doubt, and throws them over upon human enactments to learn their duty to God; so that the rebuke and reproach of God is realized. "Your fear toward me is taught by the precept of men." This base course of reasoning is not only dishonorable to God and derogatory to his Word, but it binds men hand and foot, and delivers them over in helpless uncertainty to an ecclesiastical and temporal despotism. It either plays into the hands of those who affirm that the Bible is not a book to be trusted to private judgment, but that the infallibility of the Church is the only authority and safety, and therefore the Word of God must never be consulted but by the Church's permission, nor anything found in it but what the Church declares; or it plays into the hands of civil despotisms, giving them the power to bind the conscience, to interpret God's Word, to make God's Word of none effect by their traditions, and to take away all freedom from the human mind. Either way, the moment you relinquish your hold on the supremacy of God's Word over the conscience, you make men slaves to men.

But there is another form and possession of our inheritance as important to be preserved, and for the freedom and purity of which it is quite as essential that it be regulated by the Word of God, as any of our more sacred interests, and that is, A FREE PRESS. Divine laws must sustain it, divine laws alone can preserve it from licentiousness. In this time there has arisen a power, which our fathers never contemplated, a power that may be used for as much evil as good, a power, of which it is equally difficult to define the limits, or regulate the exercise, or control the influence, or calculate the results. This power is that of the newspaper press. If we are anywhere in danger of various local despotisms in this country, it is perhaps an unprincipled editorial despotism which is to be feared, not indeed in the dominion of mind, independent and vigorous, but in the fraudful and partisan application which is made of these agencies of public opinion bearing upon it, moulding it, sometimes creating it. After the period of weakness and difficulty in the establishment of these agencies is passed, and they become wealthy and profitable by a vast subscription, they are almost irresponsible, except to the great wealth of their owners, and the means of increasing it. Besides, a journal of some fifteen or twenty thousand subscribers may speak every day, or every week, to some fifty or sixty thousand readers. If this power becomes unprincipled, immoral, or infidel, how tremendous are its facilities for the circulation of pernicious sentiments and teachings! The very subscribers, from being its patrons, as they were called when it first started, become in some sort its dependents, because by multitude they have given it an irresponsible power. For you might as well expect a combination and agreement among all the rain-drops that feed a torrent, to stop descending, when they see their brook running to the ocean, as a covenant among the subscribers of a journal, which has become wealthy and feared, and of great influence, by a circulation of twenty or thirty thousand, to cripple its energies when they see it going wrong. Hence in some cases, in large cities especially, there may be such a subjection to this power, its means of proscription are so vast, that almost the whole mercantile community may for a season be enslaved by it. If a public meeting is called to accomplish some partisan purpose, and an individual does not choose to add his name to the list of signers, forthwith he shall be marked, and if not designated plainly, shall be so pointed out, that no designation of name or profession shall be necessary, and if he will not sacrifice his principles for the sake of selling his goods, ten thousand paragraphs shall go forth concerning him, intended to break up his business and break down his independent mind. Is not this infamous?

The same game of proscription may be attempted with clergymen; but no newspaper, nor all the newspapers in the world combined, can touch the minister of Christ, or truly injure him, if he will but be faithful to his God. Besides, in some respects the tides of newspaper influence are like the waves of the ocean; each one successively chases the other out of being. Often they rise so high and furious, that you might think everything would be devoured before them; but a truly independent mind is above them, yea, rides upon them, as a noble steamer in the ocean rides on in safety, and is borne upwards and onward by the very waves that, chasing one another in such swift and furious succession, threaten to overwhelm her. She rides safely, because she minds her own helm, and not winds and waves, and because her helm is guided by her compass, and she goes on by her own machinery and internal fires. If she minded the waves and sought to avoid them by laying her course alongside, with theirs, she would soon be in the trough between seas, or wrecked and helpless at their power. Just so, an independent mind will go safely, if God's Word is at the helm, and God's Spirit in the heart; and such a man has nothing to do with the waves, but just to ride upon them.

Moreover, there is some safeguard and check upon this irresponsible power, in the country independence of the farmers, and in the local country newspapers. It is not the harbors nor the cities that can rule our globe; if they could, all hope of freedom might be swamped in the worship of Mammon and of power. But there is a spirit of independence in the country, that no combinations in the city, or in tide waters, can put down. Tide waters? tide waters? If the people, dwelling on them, measure their prosperity and their morals by their merchandise, or put their religious sentiments and principles of freedom under the law of the tides of commercial and political fluctuation, instead of the guidance and guardianship of God's Word, what hope is there for the regeneration of society? Tide waters and harbors? What would they be, without the Rivers, that water the interior of the country, pouring down from the mountains, sometimes meeting the ocean like a rival sea, and ever singing on their way the songs of the Mountain Spirit of Liberty!

Another form and possession in the inheritance of our liberties, and at the foundation of them, is A FREE AND TRUE EDUCATION, available for all, open to all, where the winds of truth blow freely across the mind, and neither civil nor hierarchical censors have power to expurgate the school-books. Our fathers began, and their system of religion and of liberty needed, such a free and universal education, at its foundations; but since the multitudinous tide of an ignorant foreign immigration, which our fathers never contemplated, we need it still more. The children of the present generation are to be the holders of a power almost beyond even our own conception, though we do stand now, where we can see the rushing and accelerating tide of population and dominion pouring on like an oceanic cataract. The children of the present generation are to determine the destinies of more than a hundred millions, and are to exert an influence on the whole world more mighty for good or evil, than the sphere of our country has ever yet comprehended. The great question for us is, Shall they be wisely educated? Shall we give to them, and to their activity and influence, now that we *can* do it, such a direction, such a character, as that, by God's blessing, the tremendous power to come into their possession shall be justly, wisely, benignly, and with true Christian patriotism, wielded? Shall they be Christian Patriots? Shall we turn the hearts of the fathers to the children, and of the children to the fathers, by a training of them in those virtuous principles, from which Divine Inspiration declares they will not, when they are old, depart? We have a mighty power even with our foreign population, even with the followers of Rome, if we will begin low enough down, and near enough to the fountain; a mighty and irresistible power, with our Sunday and public schools; for it is the admission of Romanists themselves, nay, it is their own language, that "of every one hundred Roman Catholic children who attend Protestant schools, Sabbath-schools, or day-schools, you may set down ninety-eight as clear gain to the Devil;" that is, in plain English, they become Protestants, think for themselves, read the Bible, have their consciences trained under God and his word, and become intelligent honest republicans. Indeed, there is great encouragement here, and not a child in this city, or in any of our cities or towns, ought to be left vagrant or uneducated. The magnitude and preciousness of the interests at stake would justify the appointment of a children's police and board of commissioners to look after this very thing, with power and means to put every child at school, and to give to every vagrant and destitute child a free and thorough support and training. Build schools for them now, and support them there, and you will not have to build prisons for them hereafter, and incarcerate and support them *there*. There is no one thing in which the interests, welfare, and whole destiny of our republic are so perfectly and immediately at command as this. You have power to do what you will with the nation, if you will but gather up the children; but if you let the children go, you let the nation go. Take care of the children in their helpless and destitute infancy and childhood, and even the *vagrant* children will be able to take care of the country, when you yourselves are laid in the grave.

And here we mark it as a very curious thing to read the interesting and valuable reports of the Police, concerning the multitude of juvenile thieves that prowl about our docks and make daily or nightly descents upon any articles of unguarded property that may come to hand, and to see, after an array of demonstration concerning the insecurity of such property, a proposition arrived at—to take care of—what? the children? the immortal beings whom the wealthy city leaves, by neglect, to an enforced penury and vagrancy, and to all the temptations in crime produced thereby? Not at all! Alas! how little thought for them, except of prisons, or houses of correction; but a proposition natural enough, and proper enough in its way, to take care of the property, by the establishment of a special water police!

But how much better to have a special children's police, a police of humanity, charity, and benevolent guardianship, to look after the property of the State stolen by the Enemy of souls, to take every child thus found in a training of crime and beggary, and put him under humane and heavenly influences, to make thenceforth a good child, and a wise and virtuous man out of him! Ah, we would have little need to look after other kinds of property, if this were fairly, fully, heartily done. Make your proposed water police for property a children's police, to look after immortal spirits, thus abandoned to crime, and to educate and save *them*, and all the expenses of your water and land police too would soon be more than saved to the city.

But there is a great, terrible, ominous neglect, especially in our great cities. And throughout our country there is by no means that watchfulness and faithfulness in this matter of a general education, which the very existence and security of freedom imperatively demands. For while in the New England States, and in New York and Ohio, the proportion of children educated is one out of every 4, a quarter part; in Indiana and Kentucky it is only one out of every 17, a seventeenth part; and in South Carolina it is only one out of 64, a sixty-fourth part. But in our great cities there is the greatest danger of neglect, and there the greatest guilt and misery are sure to follow.

We have noted some of the primeval and present elements of our country's prosperity and greatness. For the continuance of that prosperity and greatness, we are entirely dependent on the Divine blessing, since not one of those elements can be vital and permanent without Divine grace. And here our Pilgrim and Puritan Fathers took hold upon the promises, feeling their dependence upon God. They did not wish for a state, which should not be loyal to God; they did not think existence as a people worth having, if not obedient to him, and enjoying his presence. So they threw themselves on God, and left us, along with the causes, which their self-denying virtue and wisdom had put in operation, an inheritance of prayer, and an example of the spirit of prayer and of trust in God, worth more in God's sight than all other possessions. It was their religious spirit, more than anything else, that made this country *one* country; it is the same prayerful and religious spirit that must *keep* it one. If the spirit of faith and prayer prevails, it will be a bond of union that nothing can break; it will be the unity of the spirit in the bond of peace. To make that bond perpetual, every man's energies, far and near, should be affectionately, fervently, prayerfully bent, for the avoiding and sacrificing of every evil thing, that interferes with such union. Every wicked thing that perils it should be put down. Agitation *cannot* be put down, opinion cannot be put down. Our union would be a dead sea of stagnation if it could. Agitation and wholesome healthful excitement by all the winds of free opinion must be our life, as the very tempests of the ocean preserve it from rotting. The waves must roll and play, for we are to live the life of an active, fearless, energetic empire.

Let every man seek the things that truly make for peace, asking of the Lord God, what wilt thou have me to do? Our union is a thing of the spirit, not the form merely; and if one man and another, or one state and another, set up their specifics for union, to bind and clamp us together as by iron, not by a free and voluntary spirit, such a union could never last. It is the spirit of freedom and piety, and nothing else that can bind us together, the law of the spirit of life in Christ Jesus. As the spirit of life is all that keeps the trunk and branches of an oak in a unity of life, and if that spirit dies, part after part rots, and drops, and at length the whole falls asunder, so is it with any country when the spirit of piety and patriotism declines. All the railroads in the world, not if you could run them from the sea of Mexico to the North Pole and from Maine and California to the Rocky Mountains, nor all the electric telegraphs in the world, running in the same lines, could bind our Union, if the spirit of union should really die; no more than a great iron bolt driven through the earth's diameter could clamp our globe together, if once the law of attraction should cease. Hence the iniquity and dreadfulness of a spirit of bitterness and alienation in one part against another, and the wickedness of measures to provoke and exasperate that spirit. God in mercy save us from such strife! We are one country, and if one part suffers, another suffers with it, and should sympathise accordingly. The head cannot say to the foot I have no need of thee, nor the eye to the hand I have no need of thee, for we are all members one of another, and would to God we were all, states and individuals, members of Christ. But we cannot come to that blissful state by quarrelling, neither can we have purity by boasting perfection, nor health by concealing disease. If a cancer is to be cut out, you cannot have life by doing nothing but administering chloroform, and never attempting to probe, but always concealing the evil. If your vessel spring a leak at sea, or your pumps get choked, you cannot save the ship by concealing the leak from the crew, or keeping them away from the pumps, or setting them to picking oakum.

Oh no! Every evil must be looked in the face, and God's mercy must be sought in conquering it. No right principles must ever be sacrificed for the sake of union. If they ever are, it will be the mistaken policy of those, who digged down the charcoal foundations of the temple, in order to keep up the fires on its altars. Union is a thing that will certainly grow out of principle, if men stick to that, but without that, union will die. We want both union for the sake of principle and principle for the sake of union. Every attempt at disunion is treason, and so are many of the pretended *alarms* of disunion. It is treason and outrage any where to say, because this or that evil cannot be in a moment put down or remedied, therefore the Union is worthless. The very way to remove the evil is by maintaining and strengthening the Union. Never to the end of time could any evil in the body politic be removed, by cutting off the part where it festers, and leaving that to die; but the body must remain undivided, and the evil be most carefully and judiciously treated, till the power of health in the whole system shall, by God's blessing, overcome it.

All God's discipline is gradual with us, and ours must be so with one another. Disunion, North or South, East or West, is treason, suicide, fratricide, parricide, every evil thing in one. It is not to be thought of, and wo be to those who for political purposes have spread the cry. Our Union is the very agency on which under God and the gospel, we base the hope and power of a redemption from evil and progress in good. If you desired the Christianizing and civilization of the most degraded nation on earth, and one should answer you that the people there are so bad, that they will soon be blotted out from among the nations, would that be any consolation? You would desire them to be kept in the family of nations still, that by kind treatment, forbearance, and sending the gospel, they may be won to goodness. And just so, if there were any one of our family of states exceedingly bad and perverse, would that be any reason for the cry of disunion? In such a case, above all others, we would *not* have disunion, at any rate; for all hope of reclaiming our sister would then be gone; but the Union must continue, and by kindness, forbearance, and love, united with firmness, we shall bring her to repentance.

Our enemies abroad, and the enemies of human progress and freedom, would rejoice in nothing so much, as the dismemberment of this Union; they would rejoice to see it broken into as many separate and conflicting pieces, as there are sovereign States. They do not care a fig for freedom, but they *do* care for *power*, and they see the sceptre of power departing from themselves, and they know that if our Union continue, slavery itself will disappear, and power over the whole world will remain with us; a power of universal freedom, that all the despotisms of the old world will then be unable to withstand. Therefore, let every man seek for the things that truly make for peace, and things whereby one may edify another; but let him not think that peace cometh by concealing sin or justifying iniquity, or hardening ourselves in oppression, or setting our will and our statutes in rebellion against God's word.

As the result of all the principles, privileges, and blessings that have been enumerated, we possess in every direction a physical and material capacity and energy, that is vast, increasing, and almost irresistible; an empire of power, spreading, deepening, rising, till it begins to overshadow the globe. Our agricultural and manufacturing interests are advancing to a concentration of the production as well as the consumption of the fruits and fabrics of all climes. Our commerce sweeps the seas in every parallel of latitude and longitude, and builds cities on almost every coast. Our naval architecture takes supremacy over that of all the world. In the peaceful career of invention, our skill and ingenuity are unrivalled, and alas, our warlike propensities and powers are quite thoroughly demonstrated and acknowledged. The cultivation of the arts and sciences, with originality, profoundness, and proficiency therein, is rapidly moving onward. Our public works are stupendous, and our private buildings are becoming palaces. Yet all this empire of material power is worthless and transitory without the spiritual; if God be not honored and glorified in it, it shall pass away as a dream. There shall not be left one stone upon another that shall not be thrown down; the dragons shall hiss among these lordly structures, and their princely chambers shall be habitations for owls, if the nation out of whose bosom all these material forms of greatness grow, refuses to honor God. "FOR THE NATION AND KINGDOM THAT WILL NOT SERVE THEE SHALL PERISH; YEA, THOSE NATIONS SHALL BE UTTERLY WASTED."

O that the mantle of our fathers' piety and prayers might descend and rest upon us! O that we might possess something of their perfect freedom from private ends, something of their entire self-devotion to their country and their God! O that God would turn the hearts of the fathers to the children, and the hearts of the children to the fathers! O that we might cherish and maintain the spirit of their loyalty to their God, their jealousy for the honor of his law, the supremacy of his word, the guardianship of his institutions! O that we might have their combined hatred of human oppression, and childlike submissiveness to God's will! their self-denying endurance, their simplicity, their integrity, their incorruptible and religious patriotism! O for their spirit of faith and prayer!

That the discipline of Divine Providence in our case has been peculiarly grand, intense and blessed, it would require the stupidity and blindness of an Atheist to deny; and we find it difficult to believe that God will suffer the moral, intellectual and physical training of this people on so magnificent a scale, and with such vast and glorious objects that may be accomplished by it, utterly to fail. Nevertheless, the voice of warning issues from the sacred word, with a solemnity deepened by the fall of the chosen people of God, after a majestic training and probation of more than a thousand years. "At what instant I shall speak concerning a nation and concerning a kingdom to build and to plant it, if it do evil in my sight, that it obey not my voice, then I will repent of this good, wherewith I said I will benefit them." And the echo of this solemn declaration comes to us from the New Testament. "Behold therefore the goodness and severity of God; on them which fall, severity, but on thee goodness, if thou continue in his goodness, otherwise, thou also shalt be cut off!"

My Brethren, let us prostrate ourselves before God, and plead with him that the warnings of his Providence and Word may be heeded, and that by obedience and gratitude on our part the inheritance of our fathers' glory may be perpetuated, and God's designs of mercy fulfilled. Then shall the sublime language of the venerated and sainted Secretary of the American Board of Commissioners for Foreign Missions, the heavenly-minded Jeremiah Evarts, be more than realized. Speaking of the time when all the happy millions of this continent shall live together as brethren, adoring their Creator and Redeemer, then, said Mr. Evarts, "will be a day of glory, such as the world has never yet witnessed. As the sun rises on a Sabbath morning and travels westward from Newfoundland to the Oregon, he will behold the countless millions assembling, as if by a common impulse, in the temples with which every valley, mountain, and plain, will be adorned. The morning psalm and evening anthem will commence with the multitudes on the Atlantic coast, be sustained by the loud chorus of ten thousand times ten thousand in the valley of the Mississippi, and prolonged by the thousands of thousands on the shores of the Pacific. Throughout this wide expanse not a dissonant voice will be heard. If unhappily, there should be here and there an individual whose heart is not in unison with this divine employment, he will choose to be silent. Then the tabernacle of God will be with men. Then will it be seen and known to the universe what the religion of the Bible can do even on this side the grave, for a penitent, restored, and rejoicing world."

Let us turn to the God of our Fathers, with the prayer that all this may be accomplished. Let us strive, in humble reliance upon God's grace, to do what we can for a consummation of happiness and glory so divine. Then, here on earth with the descendants of the Pilgrims, and there in heaven with our Pilgrim Fathers, with the spirits of the just made perfect, and all the general assembly and church of the redeemed, and the innumerable company of angels, we will shout HALLELUIA! FOR THE LORD GOD OMNIPOTENT REIGNETH!

www.ingramcontent.com/pod-product-compliance
Lightning Source LLC
LaVergne TN
LVHW011127110826
845150LV00008B/2272

* 9 7 8 1 4 1 8 1 9 4 9 7 0 *